OFFICIAL
FORTNITE
THE CHRONICLE

CONTENTS

ALL ABOARD THE BATTLE BUS!

What a ride it's been, and it's only just beginning! In this book, we take a look back at the first nine seasons of Fortnite to revisit the great additions, major changes, and crazy new toys that the game delivered in its first two years. Whether you're a relatively new player looking to find out what happened before you jumped in or a veteran who has been scoring Victory Royales since the very start, you're sure to find plenty of amazing events, memories, insights, refreshers, and moments in the pages that follow. With that, grab a seat, buckle up, and let us guide you through the complete chronicle of Fortnite...so far!

THE RISE OF
FORTNITE

HOW EPIC TOOK ON THE GAMING WORLD AND WON ITS OWN VICTORY ROYALE

Fortnite's sudden and ongoing dominance of the battle royale scene wasn't just a lucky accident. Far from it: The game was built on a number of core pillars designed to make its reign unshakable, and Epic has been toiling away behind the scenes ever since the game first released to grow it into something even bigger and better.

The colorful art style and accessible gameplay aren't the only reasons people keep piling back onto the Battle Bus in record numbers, so let's break down five of the main factors that helped define this modern-day success story....

CONSTANT EVOLUTION

New things are added as often as every day, plus there are regular seasonal updates. Everything can be altered overnight—the weapon selection, the map itself, the modes on offer, even the way the game works—giving players something to look forward to.

RELENTLESS PACE

Everything in Fortnite moves fast. Matchmaking is near-instant, and games have almost no downtime from the moment you board the bus to when you check out early or manage to come out on top. Players need to be just as speedy when completing daily and weekly challenges.

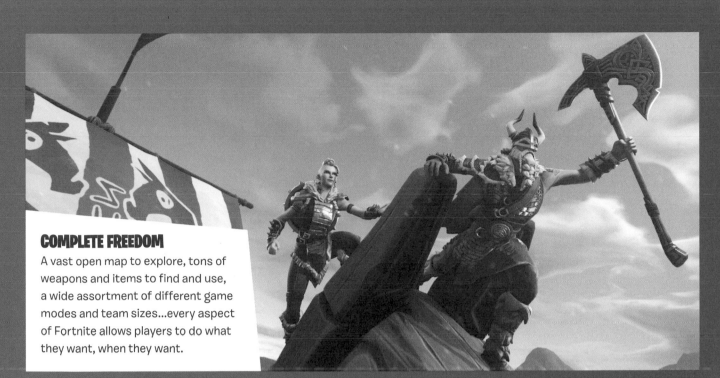

COMPLETE FREEDOM

A vast open map to explore, tons of weapons and items to find and use, a wide assortment of different game modes and team sizes...every aspect of Fortnite allows players to do what they want, when they want.

PERSONAL EXPRESSION

Just as the game is laid out in such a way that players can approach the action in whatever way they like, the varied closet of imaginative Outfits and other cool cosmetic items lets everyone express themselves visually.

BRILLIANT BUILDING

One aspect that sets Fortnite apart is the simplicity and the importance of building. This tends to be what distinguishes a great player, as they are able to throw up towers in seconds and get the high ground advantage.

SEASON 1

THE START OF SOMETHING VERY SPECIAL...

Every story has to begin somewhere, and ours takes us back to September 2017. Back then, Fortnite was known only as a cooperative survival game, pitting teams of players against undead monsters, forced to use the scraps they scavenge and their raw teamwork to fend off hordes of horrors. But, practically overnight, everything changed. Battle Royale went into Early Access on September 26, 2017, attracting millions of players to the island to seek out a Victory Royale of their own by outlasting as many other contenders as possible. Fortnite Battle Royale took the best parts of Save the World—resource management, building efficiency, and a focus on survival instincts—and put out an open invite for anyone to come and take the challenge. Weapons, map, and modes were all limited compared to today, but Fortnite would only go on to bigger and better things.

LOCKER LOOT
THE EARLY BIRD GETS THE WORM

Back in Season 1, there was no Battle Pass. Instead, the short-lived Season Shop offered exclusive purchases to players who managed to reach certain experience milestones within that period. That's why Renegade Raider remains such a popular and desirable Outfit among hardcore Fortnite fans—it hasn't yet returned to the Item Shop, and is only owned by players who put the hard work in during Fortnite's first couple of months.

Only four items were available from the Season Shop: Renegade Raider, her Revenge Harvesting Tool, and the Aerial Assault duo, consisting of a simple Outfit and Glider. Although basic, all these items hold prestige with fans.

SKULL TROOPER

Until his return in 2018's Halloween event, Skull Trooper was one of the most-wanted skins. An icon of Fortnite's first year.

PINK FLAMINGO

This novelty Harvesting Tool is always popular. Who wouldn't want to gather materials with a garish garden ornament?

ROADTRIP

The Glider has seen many reskins since Fortnite started, but this picnic blanket-themed variant is one of the smartest.

DEATH VALLEY

Strike fear into opponents with this skull-on-a-stick Harvesting Tool. It's remarkably sturdy!

SEASON 2

AND THEY SAY THAT CHIVALRY IS DEAD...

Fortnite's second season marked the beginning of the Battle Pass as we know it today, although it was a little smaller, with just 70 Tiers to work your way up through instead of the current 100. It was around this time that Epic first started to bring in alterations to the island map, adding in a bunch of new areas and making significant changes to existing ones to help keep the action as fresh as possible for regularly returning players. Biomes would also help give each area its own look and feel, something that has become increasingly prevalent in later seasons.

With more regular updates to the Item Shop and more frequent updates that added new weapons and tools to the game, it was around this time that Fortnite started to cement itself as a constantly evolving experience.

LOCKER LOOT
20,000 LIEGES UNTO THE SCENE

If you ever dreamed of securing a place at the Round Table as a noble knight, Season 2 was the place to jump in. Black Knight was the showcase Outfit as the Tier 70 Battle Pass reward, but picking up his fellow warriors on the way to the top proved to be just as rewarding. Players could grab the Blue Squire Outfit just by investing in the Battle Pass, with its female counterpart, Royale Knight, unlocking only a few Tiers later. This Battle Pass was also the only way to get hold of the now-famous Floss dance Emote, which became another easy way to spot early adopters of the game.

ESSENTIAL EXTRAS

CUDDLE TEAM LEADER

A truly iconic Outfit. Who wouldn't want to run around dressed as a giant teddy bear?

BEAR FORCE ONE

One of the cutest Gliders, this was introduced to celebrate Valentine's Day alongside the Cuddle Team Leader.

MERRY MARAUDER

This Outfit was hugely desirable after its appearance in 2017. It returned in 2018 with a female counterpart.

BLACK SHIELD

This cool dragon-crested buckler belongs to the Black Knight, and could be unlocked by reaching Tier 70 of the Battle Pass.

SEASON 3

GRAB YOUR SPACE SUIT AND AIM FOR THE STARS

If Season 2 was about looking back to the past with its medieval theme, the third season instead revolved around looking up to the skies above and the infinite vastness that lies beyond. The focus on space exploration didn't stop with all the cool cosmetics that graced the Battle Pass and the Item Shop—around halfway through the season, players began to notice meteors in the sky, with observation camps popping up shortly after the first sightings. This marked the beginning of Fortnite foreshadowing how the game might change in the future with in-game events. It all came to a head at the end of the season, with meteor showers damaging parts of the island before major impacts leveled landmarks like Dusty Depot, completely changing the map. It was also Season 3 that debuted the 100-Tier Battle Pass we have today.

LOCKER LOOT
MAKE SPACE FOR THESE STELLAR OUTFITS

Many of Season 3's Battle Pass unlockables were from the Space Explorers set, with six of the set's 15 items up for grabs for regular players. Three different astronaut costumes were available: Mission Specialist from the off to get all Battle Pass owners started; Moonwalker at Tier 55; and the gloomy Dark Voyager all the way up at Tier 70—although not all featured Outfits stuck to the space theme.... Rust Lord's getup looks better suited to the wastelands than to outer space, and Elite Agent brings a little Secret Services flair to Fortnite.

ESSENTIAL EXTRAS

REX
Crazy costumes are no rare sight now, but this Legendary dinosaur-themed Outfit was an early highlight.

BACKUP PLAN
Twitch Prime members have had quite a few free bits and pieces, with this explosive Back Bling being a standout.

ORBITAL SHUTTLE
This Glider allows wannabe astronauts to pretend they're landing on the island after an interstellar mission.

CARROT STICK
If you're on an egg hunt, this is the tool you want. It's a carrot, an egg basket, and a chocolate bunny, all rolled into one.

SEASON 4

WELCOME TO THE GOLDEN AGE OF SUPERHEROES

As Dusty Depot was blown to bits at the start of the new season, a research facility popped up in what would become known as Dusty Divot to investigate the comet that had changed the island. While scientists toiled over excavating the space rock, new factions took to the map to stake their claim on the discovery—a villain's lair appeared on the west side of the map, with a host of heroes on hand to deal with whatever

nefarious schemes might be hatched there, and later a detective agency was set up. All the while, this buzz captured the imaginations of everyone else on the island, with movie sets and a drive-in theater allowing players to feel like superstars.

Later on in the season, the villains launched a huge rocket and, once again, everything was about to change on the island....

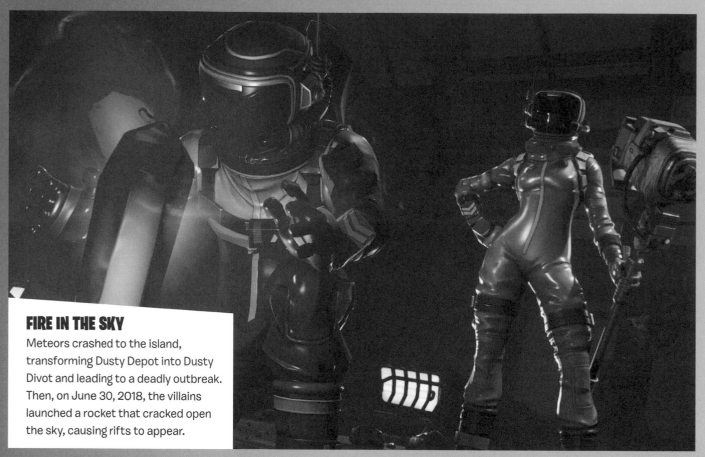

FIRE IN THE SKY

Meteors crashed to the island, transforming Dusty Depot into Dusty Divot and leading to a deadly outbreak. Then, on June 30, 2018, the villains launched a rocket that cracked open the sky, causing rifts to appear.

LEARN TO FLY

The Jetpack was introduced as a limited-time Legendary mobility option, allowing users to make short flights. It was prone to overheating, so using it sparingly was essential to avoid crashing to the ground.

CHOOSE YOUR WEAPON

New weaponry was added, including the Dual Pistols and the rarer Burst Assault Rifles, as well as the useful Thermal Scoped Assault Rifle and the Drum Gun.

FRESH FROM THE MALL

Season 4 brought with it Fortnite's first vehicle, but it wasn't as advanced as some expected. Still, the Shopping Cart allowed pairs of players to get around quickly, and paved the way for more vehicles.

THE VAULT
IN: Crossbow, Jetpack
OUT: None

STAR POWER

Epic launched the Blockbuster Contest, inviting fans to use the in-game movie sets and the game's replay feature to produce short movies. Winner Janthony picked up a cool 25,000 V-Bucks!

LOCKER LOOT
WE COULD BE HEROES, JUST FOR ONE SEASON

Carbide was the main star of Season 4, unlocked at Tier 1 of the Battle Pass, with his nemesis Omega all the way up at Tier 100. Players could also add the striking Valor Outfit to their roster of heroes along the way, as well as a bunch of other less heroic (but no less awesome) Outfits. The eyepatched Battlehawk reported for duty at Tier 1, joined later by Squad Leader. A pair of alternatives came in the form of Teknique and Zoey.

ESSENTIAL EXTRAS

FLYTRAP

This super-villain had an impish appearance, with vines creeping around his limbs as he looked to whip rivals into the dirt.

HANG TIME

We're not convinced that a basketball backboard is the most aerodynamic glider design, but it works just fine.

CONFIDENTIAL CASE

Unlocked with the Gumshoe Outfit, this lets players know that you're too busy working a case to throw down.

PARTY ANIMAL

This Harvesting Tool made from Slurp Juice is as effective at destroying things as it is restoring them!

SEASON 5

GO ON A JOURNEY THROUGH SPACE AND TIME

Past, present, and future collided after the villains managed to successfully launch their rocket and crack open the sky. Spatial rifts peppered the map, catapulting players through them high into the air—useful, sure, but someone should probably run some tests to check that's safe. As the rift problem worsened, the crack shrunk, but started spitting out lightning bolts. The most powerful of these signalled the rift's ultimate disappearance, but the strike left in its wake a strange purple cube. The community tried to make sense of this while the cube slowly made its way across the map, creating strange occurrences, zapping anyone foolish enough to shoot it, and bouncing nearby players away. Finally, it made its way to Loot Lake, corrupting the entire body of water and ushering in a new season where things would get even stranger....

IT'S PLAYTIME

Season 5 gave us a fun new extra for the Emote slot in the form of toys. Tee up the golf ball and give it a whack with your Harvesting Tool, or stop to shoot some hoops with the basketball.

HAPPY BIRTHDAY!

Fortnite celebrated its first anniversary in style, by letting everyone eat cake. As well as sweet treats, players were given a set of challenges to complete for unique rewards.

GET 'EM WHILE YOU CAN

Limited Time Modes brought new ways to play with unique game modes that only stick around for a short while—from large-scale team battles to heists and score attack challenges.

ANOMALY DETECTED

The rifts got worse over the course of the season, culminating in a lightning strike that left a mysterious cube. This moved across the map, setting up the next season.

THE VAULT

IN: Revolver, Common Suppressed SMG, Rare Rocket Launcher, Legendary Bolt-Action Sniper Rifle, Rare Pistol, Tactical SMG, Drum Gun
OUT: None

BY ODIN'S BEARD!

With the rifts playing havoc with space and time, there were many strange sights to see. Perhaps the freakiest was the Viking village that sprung up atop the waterfall at B6, complete with longboat!

LOCKER LOOT
AN OUTFIT COLLECTION FOR THE AGES

Drift was the poster boy of Season 5, with his style getting more and more elaborate as he acquired a coat and mask. At the opposite end of the Battle Pass was Ragnarok. The rest of the Outfits ranged from Redline's biker chic to Rook's field agent attire, with the Viking warrior Huntress providing a female counterpart to Ragnarok's fearsome look.

ESSENTIAL EXTRAS

WILD CARD

One of the faces of the High Stakes Limited Time Mode. You can customize the mask to display different cards.

BOOMBOX

Grab the Mullet Marauder Outfit and you'll get this along with it, letting you really bring the noise!

SHADOW PUPPET

Hacivat's Glider has a large sail doubling as a screen that plays out an odd little puppet show and weird music.

STUDDED AXE

Before Luxe's solid gold pick was added, this was the best way to add bling to your gathering. It still turns heads!

KICKING BACK AT LAZY LINKS

This luxury resort and golf course was the perfect place to chill out and play a few holes with your newly unlocked toys. It also had the benefit of being a likely spawn for the brand new All-Terrain Kart, meaning your squad could pile into the golf buggy and make a mess of the fairways.

Sadly, Lazy Links is no longer
taking reservations—it was flooded
and overrun with pirates at the start
of Season 8, and they even left their
galleon docked there, although
the crew itself is nowhere to
be seen. All the more loot
for you, though!

SEASON 6

MONSTERS ARRIVE AND THINGS GET DARK...

These were truly Fortnite's darkest days, with the mysterious cube that appeared toward the end of Season 5 continuing its reign of pandemonium. Even wilder things were in store this time, with the cube carrying an island from Loot Lake all the way around the map, collecting energy from all of the rune sites before returning to the lake and exploding, spewing monsters onto the island just in time for the appropriately named Fortnitemares event. These creatures were a decent source of extra loot, but their aggression could be a distraction: It was all too easy to get carried away slaying evil beasts, only to be picked off by another player. As this madness came to a close, players began to notice a blizzard far off the coast, which later turned out to be a gigantic iceberg on a collision course with the island. Then, it began to snow. Winter was coming....

GAME CHANGES
CORRUPTED HIGHLIGHTS

FRIENDS FOR LIFE

Pets took Back Bling to the next level. These cute animals sit on your back and react to how you perform. Three Pets were introduced, with more joining in later seasons.

GET DOWN!

Little quality-of-life changes can make a big difference in the game, and the addition of unlockable music tracks that can be played in the lobby was a fantastic new feature.

EMBRACE THE DARKNESS

Harness the Shadow Stones and you'll be unstoppable...These crystals make you hard to track, while also granting a phase ability that can warp through objects.

TIME FOR TURRETS

Sometimes, you need to bring out the big guns. The Mounted Turret lets players pilot a powerful gun emplacement with unlimited ammo.

THE VAULT

IN: Impulse Grenade, Suppressed SMG, Light Machine Gun, Bouncer, Remote Explosives, Semi-Automatic Sniper Rifle, Dual Pistols, Guided Missile
OUT: Guided Missile

AWESOME FOUR-SOME

Put the "quad" in "squad" with these new toys! The Quad Launcher fires salvos of missiles to make short work of fortified positions, while the Quad Crasher ATV smashes obstacles with ease.

LOCKER LOOT
LOOKS THAT LIGHT UP THE LAND

This season let you say howdy to Calamity, the Wild West wonder woman. Her posse is...well, *interesting*. The duo of Fable and Dire brought Red Riding Hood to life, while Dusk was ready to take a bite out of the opposition in her goth getup. And where else could you hope to find a tomato-headed assassin (Nightshade) and a robotic llama (DJ Yonder)?

ARACHNE

Few Outfits strike fear into opponents like this spider queen. Couple it with the Long Legs Back Bling for extra shudders.

FLAPPY FLYER

It's one of the goofiest Gliders in the game, but after you enter battle on a chicken, you'll never want a regular Glider!

THUNDER CRASH

Even Brite Bomber's trusty axe wasn't safe from corruption, mutating into this twisted new form.

SHACKLED STONE

Fans of this season can use Deadfire's Shackled Stone Back Bling to keep a Shadow Stone with them wherever they go.

MAP WATCH

The cube continued to roam the map during Season 6. This time, however, it was carrying a passenger—an island ripped straight from Loot Lake. This floating landmass was dragged to each rune site in turn, before it was taken back to where it came from....

ON THE MOVE!

Tracking the flying island was never difficult. It moved slowly and would often stay in one spot for days at a time as it absorbed the power of the runes. It could always be found either at or heading towards one of these corrupted sites.

SEASON 7

A COLD SNAP SWEEPS ACROSS THE ISLAND

The iceberg that was on a collision course with the island finally made contact, and everything took a decidedly frigid turn. The entire southwest corner of the map was engulfed and expanded by the mass of snow and ice, adding a bunch of new landmarks—a wintery village, an arctic airstrip, and a towering mountain that would gradually melt away slightly to reveal a majestic castle. The Ice King eventually emerged to cast a huge spell that would unleash frozen beasts all across the map. Later, the mysterious Prisoner, who had been kept deep in the castle's dungeon, escaped to do something about the unexpected ice age. Being on ice for so long had clearly dulled his powers, but it wouldn't be very long before he would bring in yet another massive round of changes with his long-dormant abilities, ushering in the next season....

GAME CHANGES
THIS SEASON'S COOLEST NEW FEATURES

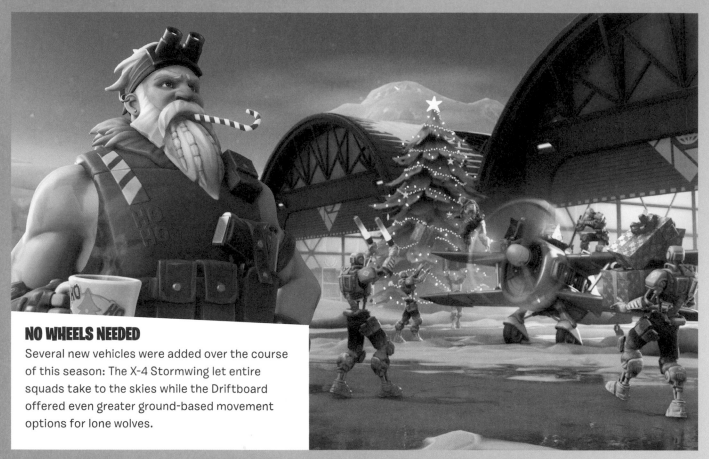

NO WHEELS NEEDED

Several new vehicles were added over the course of this season: The X-4 Stormwing let entire squads take to the skies while the Driftboard offered even greater ground-based movement options for lone wolves.

ZIPPING AROUND

With the greater verticality of the new snowy area came the need for a way for players to cross vast climbs and chasms, which is where ziplines came in handy. Don't worry—you can still fire weapons while riding these handy cables, so zip away!

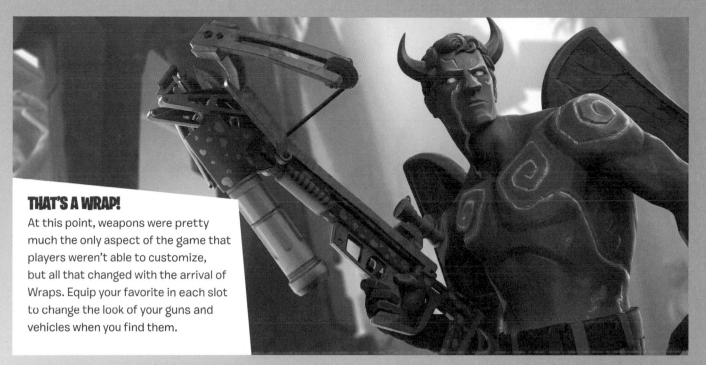

THAT'S A WRAP!

At this point, weapons were pretty much the only aspect of the game that players weren't able to customize, but all that changed with the arrival of Wraps. Equip your favorite in each slot to change the look of your guns and vehicles when you find them.

WINTER WONDERLAND

That slushy new area on the map was too significant a change not to warrant being its own discussion point. Each of the new main POIs offered its own benefits, encouraging players to land there and allowing them to check out the newest part of the island.

THE VAULT

IN: Shadow Stones, Port-A-Fort, Chiller, Clinger, Double Barrel Shotgun, Shockwave Grenade, Bolt-Action Sniper Rifle, Burst Assault Rifle, Heavy Shotgun, SMG, Grenades, Boombox
OUT: Suppressed SMG, Dual Pistols, Clingers, Cupid's Crossbow (limited)

GET CREATIVE!

The new Creative mode offered players unlimited resources with which to build cool challenges and structures, which could then be shared with others. The best builds would later be featured on the actual in-game map, in a new, regularly changing area known as The Block.

LOCKER LOOT
HOW TO WRAP UP WARM IN STYLE

Both of the Tier 1 Outfits this season reflected the chilly conditions of the new island, what with the arctic gear of Zenith and Lynx's full-cover catsuit. Trog is too stupid to notice the cold, and Sgt. Winter doesn't need sleeves to stay warm with that great big beard. And the dude in the middle? Oh, that's just the Ice King....It might be a good idea to bow.

ESSENTIAL EXTRAS

LIL WHIP

If you love ice cream, this is the Outfit for you. This little guy is ready to whip opponents into shape by any means necessary.

SQUID STRIKER

Rather than keep this alien in captivity, someone decided to strap it to a stick and hit things with it.

ARK WINGS

These fancy angel wings that come with the Ark Outfit won't help you fly, but they sure look fantastic.

WINTER'S THORN

The Ice Queen's chariot can be yours no matter your Outfit, making it easy to make an entrance befitting of royalty.

MAP WATCH
A HOME FIT FOR A KING...OR A QUEEN

MAP WATCH

The entire snowy section of the map was an awesome addition, but the castle atop its highest peak was the must-see attraction. It wasn't always so easy to see, however, as it slowly emerged from the tip of the iceberg once it melted away at the start of Season 7. This gradually allowed access deeper into the massive fortress and later the surrounding areas as well.

49

BRAIN FREEZE
Don't hang around in the confusing corridors beneath the castle for too long when the Storm is closing in. Many of the loot-packed chambers below the castle are built right into the ice of the mountain, which can make a timely escape difficult if you get too greedy down there!

SEASON 8

HOIST THE MAINSAIL AND SET COURSE FOR BOOTY!

The Prisoner escaped from the Ice King's castle and brought fire and flame to the island in the form of a huge erupting volcano. The loot-packed temples of Sunny Steps also brought bands of pirates to the island in search of riches, and they were even good enough to leave a few of their toys for you to play with! Pirate forts popped up around the map, where players could scavenge leftover loot, while a lucky few would manage to get their hands on maps that would lead to an entire arsenal of Legendary gear. The volcano that appeared near where Wailing Woods used to be proved to be a hotbed for action and gear, and escaping with your goodies was made even easier by the geysers that surrounded the lava-soaked area. Season 8 also brought with it a different vehicle lineup, with several former staples left in the garage as the Baller took center stage.

GAME CHANGERS
THINGS ARE REALLY HEATING UP ON THE ISLAND....

VOLCANO

The emergence of a huge volcano in the northeast corner of the map brought with it some tasty loot and geysers that acted as natural Launch Pads to blast players skywards.

STEP TO IT

Sunny Steps was a new city that emerged at the edge of what used to be Wailing Woods. Standing at the bottom of the Fiery Volcano, you'll discover pyramids, temples and loot galore!

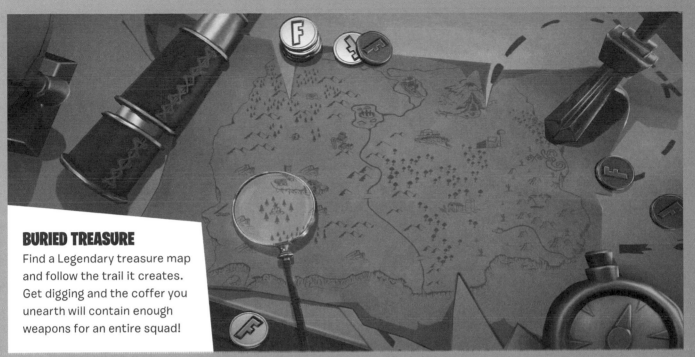

BURIED TREASURE

Find a Legendary treasure map and follow the trail it creates. Get digging and the coffer you unearth will contain enough weapons for an entire squad!

PIRATE FORTS

As well as their flagship galleon, the pirates left small encampments all around the map with plenty of treasure chests available.

THE VAULT

IN: Bottle Rockets, Chiller Grenade, Sneaky Snowman, All-Terrain Kart, X-4 Stormwing, Shopping Cart
OUT: Impulse Grenade

CATCH A DRIFT

With the weather heating up, the map's snowy southwest shrank a touch, but there were still plenty of opportunities to catch air, pull tricks and battle enemies on the supercool Driftboard.

LOCKER LOOT
WEAR THE WILD THING, ARRRRRR!

Luxe is the look if bling is your thing. The Legendary tier 100 skin has four color options and if you're going for gold you'll need to outlast 25,000 opponents! Sidewinder is coiled and ready to strike as part of the Snakepit kit, while Hybrid unleashes the dragon with his Brood kit. You're sure to want to unlock Master Key's masked style and then there's Blackheart—this piratical rogue has a dash of swashbuckling flair.

LITTLE EXTRAS

CUDDLE DOLL

Grab the Nightwitch Outfit and you'll get this voodoo doll Back Bling to show your distaste for all things cuddly.

SUNRISE

The Sun Soldiers set offers a bunch of Aztec-style Outfits and accessories, perfect for exploring the jungles.

FLIMSIE FLAIL

Find Twistie and Bendie a little over-the-top? Grab this Harvesting Tool for slightly more subdued blow-up fun.

BOOTY BUOY

What better way to descend onto the island than in the company of a confused octopus and tons of treasure?

MAP WATCH
DIVE IN AT LAZY LAGOON

GET SHIPSHAPE

The galleon in Lazy Lagoon was a great place to drop in, with a vast amount of loot on board the ship itself, on the beaches, and in the nearby port town. Cannons in the ship's underbelly can be used to bombard enemies or escape danger if your sweet landing zone turns sour.

IT'S A TRAP!
Sure, that chest in the crow's nest looks tempting, but all of the good stuff plummets to the deck below. Better have some Gliders or building materials ready to break your fall....

THE HEAT IS ON
ADVENTURE TIME AT SUNNY STEPS

STEP IT UP
Sunny Steps's Aztec theme makes for a striking location with a giant pyramid dominating the city and the lava-spitting volcano looming above it all. Treasure chests are dotted all around the area so be sure to explore thoroughly.

BALLER

These rideable globes only fit one person and the driver can't use weapons or items, but they offer protection and there's an extra trick in the grapple gun.

BOOM BOW

This explosive longbow only comes in Legendary rarity. It takes out unshielded players just by landing an arrow near them and fully-charged hits will wipe anybody out.

PIRATE CANNON

Want to make some serious impact? Pirate Cannons are found around the map and will deal out a stunning 100 damage on foes with a direct hit and a still-impressive 50 to any enemies who are unlucky enough to be within the radius. Boom!

SEASON 9

GET READY FOR A FUTURE SHOCK...

We should have known that volcano wouldn't stay dormant for long, but nobody could have foreseen the widespread damage across the map that was caused by the inevitable eruption.

While Jonesy took shelter in an underground bunker and developed a taste for bananas, others were hard at work rebuilding the affected areas. When he emerged (with a beard down to his ankles), the future had come early. Several key locations got hi-tech renovations, and other futuristic elements such as floating bases and transport tubes started peppering the map. Meanwhile, airships and other hovering vehicles patrolled the skies. As all this crazy new tech sprung up, the polar area started to show signs of cracking and melting, suggesting yet another set of major changes coming to the island soon....

GAME CHANGERS
THE RELENTLESS MARCH OF TECHNOLOGY CONTINUES

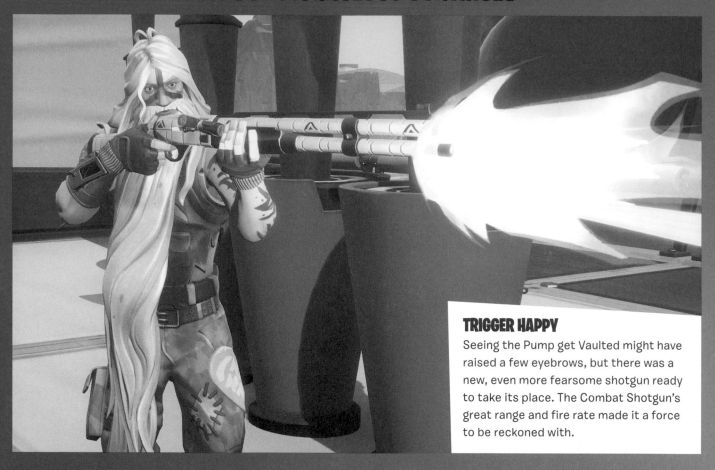

TRIGGER HAPPY

Seeing the Pump get Vaulted might have raised a few eyebrows, but there was a new, even more fearsome shotgun ready to take its place. The Combat Shotgun's great range and fire rate made it a force to be reckoned with.

GET SOME AIR!

Getting around the map has never been easier with the help of these handy slipstreams, which circle several key locations on the map and connect others. You can even fire yourself out of the wind tunnel and pull out your Glider if you need to make a quick getaway.

DON'T LOOK DOWN

High in the sky, a number of floating platforms appeared over the map, with vertical wind tunnels allowing them to be reached or escaped easily. With frequent chest spawns and often plenty of ground loot as well, these sky bases proved popular landing spots for folks who wanted to gear up early.

POWER PLAY

After the volcano erupted, the lava-filled crater was converted to a brand-new power plant location, which appears to provide fuel to the new hi-tech locations around the map. Don't think that the last of the lava is any less dangerous than before, though!

THE VAULT

IN: Clinger, Buried Treasure, Suppressed Assault Rifle, Balloons, Poison Dart Trap, Scoped Revolver, Thermal Scoped Assault Rifle, Pump Shotgun
OUT: Grenade

REWARDS BYTE BACK

Fortbytes were introduced as a novel way of mixing up the usual loading screen Challenges. One hundred of these chips make up one big picture, each being unlocked in different ways, from leveling up the Battle Pass or solving riddles around the map.

LOCKER LOOT
THE HOTTEST FASHION FROM THE ISLAND

We never knew we wanted a mechanical chicken Outfit until we were given one in the form of Sentinel at Tier 1 of the Battle Pass. Joined by the evolving Rox and her ever more advanced tech, Season 9 was off to a good start. The rest of the Outfits are just as cool, and each came with their own set of Challenges to unlock even more goodies. From the epic beard of Bunker Jonesy to the crimson chic of Demi, all are great additions to the Locker, with Tier 100 Outfit Vendetta being the icing on the cake.

GRIND
A robot that comes as a set with Clutch as part of the Hang Time bundle. Smash those Challenges to unlock new styles!

ASSAULT BOMBER
The Stormwings may have been put back in the hangar, but this fighter-turned-Glider will fill the void.

SPECTRAL SPINE
Give any look a creepy twist with this ghostly glowing spinal Back Bling, unlocked along with the Cryptic Outfit.

WEB WRECKER
Lean into this season's tech theme with this advanced axe, purpose-built for smacking the 1s and 0s out of anything.

CITY OF THE FUTURE

The volcano explosion may have destroyed most of the previous loot hot spot, but Fortnite's premier urban area lives on in the form of Neo Tilted. It went from punk hotspot to cyberpunk supercity almost overnight, with neon lights, video billboards, transport tubes, and advanced constructions as far as the eye can see. It's now an even cooler place to land than it was before, so get exploring and see what it has to offer....

SCI-FI SHOPPING
Tilted Towers wasn't the only location to get a futuristic makeover—Retail Row, damaged by the volcano eruption, was also transformed into the hi-tech Mega Mall.

FUTURISTIC FUN
EVEN MORE NEW WAYS TO PLAY

THE GRIND IS REAL

A downhill jam like never before! In Downtown Drop, 16 players slide down an urban street course, aiming to collect the many coins scattered along the way. Fast-paced, crazy, and totally original, this bizarre mode is one that we hope returns at some point—it's a completely different way to play Fortnite!

PERPLEXING PUZZLES

Hunting down Fortbytes can often be done solo, but sometimes a coordinated team is required to solve the puzzles that lay in wait around the island. With more clues popping up over the course of the season, players needed to be ready to team up and tackle these tasks if they wanted to grab the lot.

IN THE SHADOWS

Shadow Stones may be consigned to the Vault for the foreseeable future, but the new Shadow Bomb item is the next best thing. It doesn't offer the warp move of the corrupted crystal, instead allowing users ninja-like reflexes for a short time by enabling double-jumps and wall jumps while also cloaking them.

BREAKING THE SILENCE

As the old Suppressed Assault Rifle was bundled into the Vault, a new, less quiet version joined the game's arsenal. The Tactical Assault Rifle is a halfway house between rifles and SMGs, with a tight recoil pattern making it more effective at close range than its peers but less damaging at greater distances.

EVEN MORE CREATIVE

In keeping with the technology theme, Creative mode was updated to offer players tools to use. Floating castles, high-tech towers, neon billboards... you name it, it's probably there, waiting to be used. Nine seasons in and Fortnite keeps evolving. Where will it go next? You'll have to keep playing to find out...

ARE YOU THE ULTIMATE FORTNITE FAN?

PROVE YOU'RE WORTHY OF A VICTORY ROYALE WITH THIS TRICKY QUIZ!

COMMON

1. Which mode came first—Battle Royale or Save the World?

2. When you win a match of Fortnite, it's called a "Winner, Winner, Chicken Dinner"—true or false?

3. By which name was the location Dusty Divot previously known?

4. Can you name this emote?

5. How many players can be found in a full match of Battle Royale?

UNCOMMON

6. Fortnite Battle Royale launched in which month of 2017—March, July, September, or December?

7. How many points does a Small Shield Potion add to your shield bar?

8. Name this Outfit!

9. What's the name of the supermarket chain found in Retail Row and Tilted Towers?

10. Which famous rapper set the record for views on a Twitch stream of Fortnite?

RARE

11. Can you name this location from the game?

12. In which year was Fortnite originally revealed?

13. Which reward was unlocked at Tier 100 of the Season 5 Battle Pass?

14. What's the largest amount of V-Bucks you can buy in the store?

15. You have six different slots in your inventory—true or false?

16. Here's an Outfit, but can you identify it?

17. On what date did Season 4 officially end?

18. Which pickaxe skin was added to Fortnite as a tribute to Ninja?

19. Can you name this emoji?

20. What was given out as a reward for completing all of the Fortnite's First Birthday challenges?

WHAT KIND OF FORTNITER ARE YOU?

0-5
Common Rookie
Back to the drawing board

6-10
Uncommon Pro
Rising through the ranks

11-15
Rare Raider
All that grinding is paying off

16-20
Epic Marksman
You have an expert eye for facts!

21-25
Legendary Legend
Congratulations—your Fortnite knowledge is unmatched!

LEGENDARY

21. What inscription is written on the side of the Minigun weapon?

22. To which set does this pickaxe belong?

23. On which tier of Season 3's Battle Pass could you unlock the Moonwalker Outfit?

24. What did you have to leap through to complete the challenges in week four of Season 5?

25. There are lots of named locations in Battle Royale—but exactly how many?

HEADLINE PUBLISHING GROUP
An Hachette UK Company
Carmelite House
50 Victoria Embankment
London, EC4 0DZ
www.headline.co.uk www.hachette.co.uk

Little, Brown and Company
Hachette Book Group
1290 Avenue of the Americas, New York, NY 10104
Visit us at hbgusa.com/fortnite

www.epicgames.com

First Edition: August 2019
First U.S. Edition: October 2019
Little, Brown and Company is a division of Hachette Book Group, Inc.
The Little, Brown name and logo are trademarks of Hachette Book Group, Inc.
The publisher is not responsible for websites (or their content) that are not owned by the publisher.
ISBNs: 978-0-316-53027-9 (paper over board)
978-0-316-53028-6 (ebook), 978-0-316-53030-9 (ebook), 978-0-316-53032-3 (ebook)
U.S. edition printed in the United States of America
All images © Epic Games, Inc.
WOR
UK Hardback: 10 9 8 7 6 5 4 3 2 1
U.S. Paper Over Board: 10 9 8 7 6 5 4 3 2 1